Jacques is an artist who likes to be thought of as unusual. He lives a very happy life in his studio, painting beautiful pictures of fruit and vegetables, and enjoying the company of his pet monkey, Juliette. But Monsieur Michel, the art gallery owner, wants something different. Something with more colour, more emotion, something more *modern*. When he arrives at Jacques' studio one day, he is amazed at what he sees—however, all is not *quite* as it seems ...

what my customers want!"

Chapter 1.

A cheeky, long-tailed monkey called Juliette was not everyone's idea of a great pet. A cheeky long-tailed monkey, that was an expert at spitting out peanuts and hanging upside down from the rafters, astonished most people. But to Jacques Le Bleu, Juliette was the best pet he could wish for.

Jacques Le Bleu was an artist. During the day, he wore a pale blue artist's smock and a large pink and green polka dot bow-tie.

Every morning, Jacques filled Juliette's food bowl with peanuts, and every evening, they ate the fruit and vegetables that Jacques loved to paint.

Juliette, The Modern Art Monkey

Written by Susan Griffiths
Illustrated by Rex Lightfoot

Contents | Page

Nelson
an International Thomson Publishing company ITP®

Juliette,
The Modern Art Monkey

With these characters ...

Jacques

Monsieur Michel

Juliette

"These are exactly

At night-time, he wore pink and green floral pyjamas, with tartan slippers. He always wore his grey artist's beret, even in bed! Jacques liked people to think he was unusual, and a vegetarian artist with a peanut-spitting, rafter-hanging, cheeky, long-tailed monkey was just about as unusual as you could get!

Jacques and Juliette lived in an artist's studio, over the top of a French bakery in Paris. Their walls were covered with paintings that Jacques had almost finished. In the middle of the studio, there was a huge wooden table covered with paints, paintbrushes, marker pens, chalk, and rolled-up pieces of canvas. The whole room smelled of a curious mixture of freshly baked bread, fruit and vegetables, croissants, paint and turpentine.

Each week, Monsieur Michel, who owned the local art gallery, would visit Jacques and Juliette.

He would look at Jacques' latest paintings, sadly brush his moustache, and shake his head.

"No, no, no! Not enough people are buying paintings of bowls of fruit and vegetables anymore. Why don't you try some modern art, Jacques? That sells for a lot more money these days."

But Jacques would shake his head, too.

"Monsieur Michel, I *like* painting bowls of fruit and vegetables. No-one can paint a bowl of fruit and vegetables better than Jacques Le Bleu!"

Juliette would chatter in agreement, as she picked her way through her bowl of peanuts.

"Besides," Jacques added. "Juliette and I get to *eat* what we paint. We can't eat squiggles, strokes and dots!"

Monsieur Michel shrugged his shoulders, and brought out his cheque book. He knew he could always sell a few of Jacques' fruit bowl paintings each week, so he bought what Jacques had painted. But what he really wanted was a spectacular new style that would bring him fame and fortune. Like every art gallery owner, Monsieur Michel wanted to be the first to discover the next Picasso, Monet or Dali.

In the meantime, they had to sell nice, but unspectacular, paintings. That was how Monsieur Michel and Jacques made their living.

Day after day, Jacques got dressed, pulling his artist's smock and bow-tie over his beret.

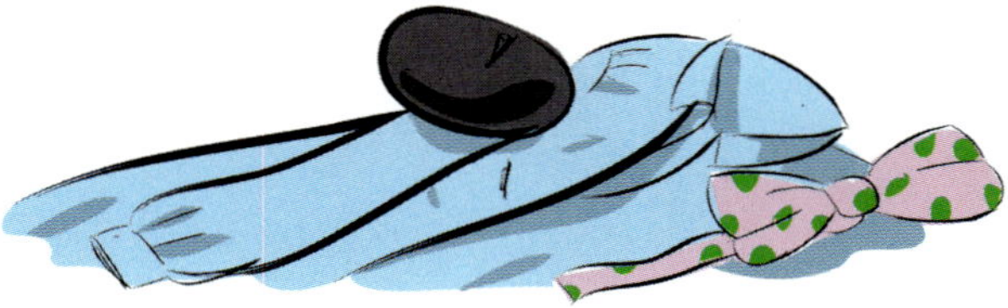

He painted his beautiful, but unspectacular, paintings. As long as Juliette had plenty of peanuts to play with, she was happy chattering to herself. She knew that, once Jacques had finished a painting, they would have the rest of the day free to play. The artist's studio was comfortable, and both Jacques and Juliette were happy with their lives.

One day, as Jacques was returning from his weekly visit to the fruit and vegetable shop, he met Monsieur Michel outside his door. He wanted to see what Jacques had painted that week.

"Hello, Jacques!"

"Hello, Monsieur Michel!"

After they greeted each other, they climbed the stairs to Jacques' studio. But when they reached the top of the stairs and opened the door, Jacques couldn't believe his eyes.

He stared in horror at the sight in the studio. Jacques was speechless.

"My goodness!" exclaimed Monsieur Michel, when he looked through the doorway.

Chapter 2.

The studio looked like a hurricane had struck. Half-full paint tubes lay all over the desk. Paint brushes and pencils lay scattered all over the floor. But, worst of all, the canvases that Jacques had carefully laid out to dry no longer looked like paintings of fruit and vegetables.

Covered in multi-coloured splotches and splashes of paint, the canvases were now ruined. Above the mess, from the rafters, hung Juliette. She swung over the paintings with a cheeky grin on her face. She was holding out an empty peanut bowl.

"Oh, no," thought Jacques. "I forgot to fill the peanut bowl this morning. She was searching for her peanuts."

Hurriedly, he scrabbled through his pockets for some peanuts, and found a couple of shells. Juliette grabbed them greedily and started to peel off the wrinkly shells to get at her favourite nuts.

Jacques had almost recovered his voice and was about to apologise to Monsieur Michel, when Monsieur Michel turned to him with a most incredulous look.

"Well done, my fine artist friend! They are magnificent!" he beamed. He was carefully examining the canvases that lay covered with paint splotches, all over the table.

"But ...," stammered Jacques in confusion.

"These are *exactly* what my customers want!" said Monsieur Michel excitedly. He rubbed his hands together and looked absolutely delighted. He looked closer at the canvases.

"The expression in these strokes is wonderful!" said Monsieur Michel enthusiastically. "The emotion is fantastic. The colours are just ... ouch!"

A peanut hit Monsieur Michel on the forehead.

Finally, Jacques recovered his voice.

"Juliette!" he said sternly.

"Never mind," said Monsieur Michel, waving his hand at Jacques. "I must have these paintings. I simply must!"

He reached into his pocket and brought out a cheque book. With a flourish, he scribbled out the cheque and handed it to Jacques.

"I'm going to pay you double your normal fee," he said excitedly. "I must rush!" Monsieur Michel gathered up the canvases, tucked them under his arms, and left in a flash.

Jacques looked at the cheque and almost fainted. It was more money than he had been paid for twenty of his fruit bowl paintings! It was too late to protest and tell the truth about what had happened. He heard Monsieur Michel clumping his way eagerly down the creaky stairs.

“I must frame these immediately,” he was whispering to himself. “My clients will pay a fortune to own a genuine Le Bleu masterpiece.”

As Monsieur Michel scurried back to his gallery, he was mentally calculating how much money he would make.

Chapter 3.

After Jacques had tidied the studio, he walked nervously down to Monsieur Michel's art gallery to explain the truth.

At the art gallery, Monsieur Michel was admiring the framed paintings hanging on the wall. A tall man was looking at the paintings enthusiastically and had started to write out a cheque. He was buying one of Juliette's paintings!

"But, Monsieur Michel, they're *not* my paintings," whispered Jacques in a worried voice. "I need to explain."

"Are you telling me that someone *else* did these paintings?" whispered Monsieur Michel, as he put the tall man's cheque in the cash register.

"Well ...," started Jacques.

"A friend of yours, perhaps?" asked Monsieur Michel eagerly.

"Well, sort of," replied Jacques. He was about to explain when Monsieur Michel clapped his hands and grinned.

"A-ha!" he said. "An artist friend of yours who wishes to remain anonymous! I *completely* understand."

"Well, not exactly ...," began Jacques. But Monsieur Michel would hear no more. He loved the idea of a mystery artist. It would make even more people talk about the paintings, and that would mean they would become even more collectable. He raised his hand.

"Don't worry, Jacques," he said. "I shall protect your friend's identity. You have my word! Besides," he added, "a mysterious, anonymous artist is great for business. My clients will be delighted! This is wonderful. I must raise the price of the paintings before I sell any more."

Monsieur Michel bustled Jacques out of his gallery. When he rushed back in to wrap up the tall man's painting, he told him the news about the new, mysterious artist he had discovered.

Jacques stood outside on the pavement and gulped. This had not gone the way he had planned. He could tell that Monsieur Michel was not interested in hearing any more.

Jacques slowly dragged his feet back to the studio.

Chapter 4.

Another day passed, but Jacques felt guilty about what had happened. How could he let Monsieur Michel sell a *monkey's* paintings? It was just not right. Even though Monsieur Michel would be disappointed that he had not discovered the latest Picasso, Monet or Dali, Jacques knew he had to tell him the truth. After he put Juliette's collar and lead on, they both headed down to Monsieur Michel's art gallery.

A tiny bell tinkled as Jacques and Juliette opened the door to Monsieur Michel's gallery.

"How good to see you! Has our anonymous artist painted any more magnificent art?" asked Monsieur Michel with an eager smile.

He waved his arm toward the empty wall behind him.

"As you see, I have sold *every* painting!"

"Actually, I have brought the real artist for you to meet," sighed Jacques.

Monsieur Michel looked excited and peered out his gallery window. When he could see no-one outside, he looked puzzled. Then, he stared at Jacques and slowly beamed a huge smile.

"A-ha!" he winked. "So it *was* you, Jacques Le Bleu. I *thought* it was. Incredible!"

Jacques shook his head.

"No, Monsieur Michel," he said. He tilted his head towards Juliette, who chattered cheekily at Monsieur Michel.

Slowly, Monsieur Michel's eyes widened as he realised what Jacques meant. His huge smile disappeared and his moustache quivered.

"Jacques Le Bleu! Are you telling me that my clients have paid thousands of francs for paintings by ... by a *monkey*?"

He looked at Juliette incredulously. Jacques just nodded. Monsieur Michel looked like he was going to faint.

“I’m ruined!” he said. “When people find out, I will be called a fraud and a liar. The whole art world will laugh at me!” Monsieur Michel wailed and ground his teeth together. He was very upset.

“I’m terribly sorry,” said Jacques. “I tried to tell you, but ...”

“You had better leave, Jacques,” interrupted Monsieur Michel. He pointed at Juliette. “If anyone sees you ... and our *artist* here, they may become suspicious.” He groaned again. “I need time to think.”

Jacques didn’t know what to say to make Monsieur Michel feel better. He hurried out the door, with Juliette chattering happily behind him. This was terrible. Now he was in trouble, and Monsieur Michel would be in even bigger trouble, all because of a simple misunderstanding. Jacques was very unhappy.

Chapter 5.

A week passed. Jacques locked himself in his studio. He didn't even bother to get changed into his artist's smock. He wore his pyjamas all day and his beret sagged. He couldn't bear to paint. Juliette tried to comfort him by not spitting so many peanuts around the room. But nothing worked. Jacques felt very sorry for Monsieur Michel and for the trouble he had caused.

Finally, he worked up the courage to visit Monsieur Michel again. After all, Monsieur Michel had been a good friend, and he deserved a proper apology. Jacques wanted to see if there was something he could do to make things better.

He put on his artist's going-out smock, left Juliette with a handful of peanuts, and walked to Monsieur Michel's gallery. When Jacques saw the gallery, he was alarmed.

The gallery had a huge black curtain drawn across the window. Monsieur Michel was standing outside on the pavement, talking to the man who Jacques had seen buying Juliette's first painting. Monsieur Michel looked very sad. He dabbed tears from his eyes, and his moustache flopped. He wore a a black arm band on the sleeve of his dark suit. The other man looked very solemn, too.

"What has happened?" asked Jacques breathlessly, as he rushed up to the pair. "Has somebody died?"

"Alas!" wailed Monsieur Michel, clapping a hand to his forehead. "Something far worse!"

The other man shook his head and looked very glum.

"This is Monsieur Bordeaux," said Monsieur Michel, introducing Jacques to the man. "He is one of my oldest and best clients," he said. Monsieur Bordeaux nodded to Jacques, who was wondering what was going on.

"I was just explaining to Monsieur Bordeaux the *terrible* tragedy that has occurred. The *tragedy* with our mystery artist," he said.

Jacques looked puzzled.

"But ...," he said. Monsieur Michel swiftly nudged him with his elbow.

"Don't say *anything*, Jacques," he said, waving his arms about. "No words can express the sadness we feel. But, if our artist feels he must *emigrate* to *Australia*, we can do nothing to stop him. It is our great loss. It is Australia's great gain!"

Jacques was hopelessly confused. Australia? What *was* Monsieur Michel talking about?

"If only Australia wasn't so far away!" added Monsieur Michel, turning his face in Jacques' direction, away from Monsieur Bordeaux. Monsieur Michel gave Jacques a tiny wink and a furious frown.

Monsieur Michel turned back to Monsieur Bordeaux and wrung his hands hopelessly.

"Well, there is nothing I can say to persuade him to stay in France. After this week, we will have no more paintings from our new artist."

"A tragedy," agreed Monsieur Bordeaux. "But, at least we have a few paintings that will become even more valuable now."

Monsieur Michel nodded and pretended to look even more distressed. Monsieur Bordeaux shook Monsieur Michel's hand and walked off down the street, leaving Jacques and Monsieur Michel alone outside the gallery.

"Emigrate?" said Jacques. "Australia?"

Chapter 6.

"Shhh!" hissed Monsieur Michel, looking left and then right, to check no-one was watching. Then he grasped Jacques by the elbow and hurried inside the gallery.

"My clients are happy because their paintings will increase in value. I am happy because my reputation will not be ruined. And *you* should be happy because I have got you out of serious trouble!" smiled Monsieur Michel. He rubbed his hands together.

"Now, where is that monkey of yours? We still have a few days before our 'artist' is due to 'emigrate'. How many more paintings can she do?"

But Jacques shook his head. He didn't want any more trouble.

"No, Monsieur Michel. We can't do that. I'm afraid Juliette's career as an 'artist' is over."

Monsieur Michel sighed and shrugged his shoulders.

"I suppose you're right. We should quit while we're ahead."

Monsieur Michel looked over at the bare wall in his gallery where Juliette's paintings had been displayed. They were all gone. Then he smiled and slapped Jacques on the back.

He knew he would have to wait a little longer before he discovered the next Picasso, Monet or Dali. But life had to go on.

"Well, Jacques, I still need some paintings to sell, so I suppose it will be back to business as usual."

Jacques was relieved. Business as usual. That sounded just fine to him. He shook Monsieur Michel's hand and walked around the corner to the fruit and vegetable shop.

There, he bought the freshest fruit and vegetables he could find—and an extra large bag of peanuts.

There was work to do—and a cheeky, peanut-spitting, rafter-hanging monkey to keep out of trouble!

"A Modern Art Monkey."

There once was an artist from Paris,
Whose monkey was determined to embarrass,
With paint she did splash,
And was offered lots of cash,
For all of her modern art canvas!